A LETTER FROM PETER MUNK

Since we started the Munk Debates, my wife, Melanie, and I have been deeply gratified at how quickly they have captured the public's imagination. From the time of our first event in May 2008, we have hosted what I believe are some of the most exciting public policy debates in Canada and internationally. Global in focus, the Munk Debates have tackled a range of issues, such as humanitarian intervention, the effectiveness of foreign aid, the threat of global warming, religion's impact on geopolitics, the rise of China, and the decline of Europe. These compelling topics have served as intellectual and ethical grist for some of the world's most important thinkers and doers, from Henry Kissinger to Tony Blair, Christopher Hitchens to Paul Krugman, Peter Mandelson to Fareed Zakaria.

The issues raised at the Munk Debates have not only fostered public awareness, but they have also helped many of us become more involved and, therefore, less intimidated by the concept of globalization. It is so easy to be inward-looking. It is so easy to be xenophobic. It is so easy to be nationalistic. It is hard to go into the unknown. Globalization, for many people, is an abstract concept at best. The purpose of this debate series is to help people feel more familiar with our fast-changing world and more comfortable participating in the universal dialogue about the issues and events that will shape our collective future.

I don't need to tell you that there are many, many burning issues. Global warming, the plight of extreme poverty, genocide, our shaky financial order: these are just a few of the critical issues that matter to people. And it seems to me, and to my foundation board members, that the quality of the public dialogue on these critical issues diminishes in direct proportion to the salience and number of these issues clamouring for our attention. By trying to highlight the most important issues at crucial moments in the global conversation, these debates not only profile the ideas and opinions of some of the world's brightest thinkers, but they also crystallize public passion and knowledge, helping to tackle some of the challenges confronting humankind.

I have learned in life—and I'm sure many of you will share this view—that challenges bring out the best in us. I hope you'll agree that the participants in these debates challenge not only each other but also each of us to think clearly and logically about important problems facing our world.

Peter Munk (1927–2018)
Founder, Aurea Foundation
Toronto, Ontario

Published in Canada in 2019 and the USA in 2019 by House of Anansi Press Inc.
www.houseofanansi.com

23 22 21 20 19   1 2 3 4 5

Library and Archives Canada Cataloguing in Publication

Title: The rise of populism : Bannon vs. Frum : the Munk debates / edited by
Rudyard Griffiths.
Names: Bannon, Stephen K., panelist. | Frum, David, 1960– panelist. |
Griffiths, Rudyard, editor.
Series: Munk debates.
Description: Series statement: The Munk debates
Identifiers: Canadiana (print) 20189060905 | Canadiana (ebook) 20189060913 |
ISBN 9781487006297 (softcover) | ISBN 9781487006303 (EPUB) |
ISBN 9781487006310 (Kindle)
Subjects: LCSH: Populism. | LCSH: World politics—21st century.
Classification: LCC JC423 .R57 2019 | DDC 320.56/62—dc23

Library of Congress Control Number: 2018962115

Canada Council
for the Arts

Conseil des Arts
du Canada

ONTARIO ARTS COUNCIL
CONSEIL DES ARTS DE L'ONTARIO
an Ontario government agency
un organisme du gouvernement de l'Ontario

*We acknowledge for their financial support of our publishing program
the Canada Council for the Arts, the Ontario Arts Council,
and the Government of Canada.*

Printed and bound in Canada

THE RISE OF POPULISM

STEPHEN K. BANNON VS. DAVID FRUM

THE MUNK DEBATES

Edited by Rudyard Griffiths

ANANSI

CONTENTS

Pre-Debate Interviews with Moderator
Rudyard Griffiths

STEPHEN K. BANNON IN CONVERSATION WITH RUDYARD GRIFFITHS

RUDYARD GRIFFITHS: Steve Bannon, thank you for coming to Toronto for the Munk Debates.

STEPHEN BANNON: Thank you for having me.

RUDYARD GRIFFITHS: Great to have you here. You're an important global participant in the conversation about populism. I want to start by defining some terms. Tonight's debate is about whether the future — the political future of the West — belongs to populism or liberalism. What kind of populist are you? Are you a small-*d* democrat populist, a capital-*r* Republican populist, a capital-*a* Anarchist populist? Help me understand the populism of Steve Bannon.

STEPHEN BANNON: Our populism is tied to economic nationalism. The movement in the United States—and the one that I am associated with worldwide—is anti-elite. We believe that what I call the "Party at Davos"—this kind of scientific, engineering, managerial, financial, cultural elite—has taken the world in the wrong direction, buying into globalization to the detriment of the "little guy." And so this is really a representation of anti-elitism, and really about having the little guy get a piece of the action. As conservative or right-wing populists, we believe in economic nationalism; "America First" national security—which is not isolationism, but America *first*; and what I call the deconstruction of the administrative state, to take apart the Leviathan, this all-encompassing state that we've got in the United States. So we're definitely not anarchists or libertarians, but we're very anti-elite.

RUDYARD GRIFFITHS: Where did this all come from? To the casual observer, it seems as if in the last twenty-four to thirty-six months, populism has gone off like a flashbang grenade around the world. But you think it has older antecedents—a longer, delayed fuse that has ignited. Take us back through that story.

STEPHEN BANNON: In story terms, the "inciting incident" is clearly the financial crisis of 2008. Now, many of these issues were around before then, but I think that's the thing that really drove it. In the financial collapse of 2008, brought on by the elites—among which no one's ever been held accountable—what you had was really the elites taking care of themselves. Essentially what they did was just create money. They flooded the zone with a fancy term we call "liquidity." The balance sheet of the Federal Reserve was about $880 billion on the day of the financial crash, September 18, 2008. When Trump took office in January 2017, it was $4.5 trillion.

That money lifted up asset holders—stocks, bonds, real estate assets, hedge funds, investment banks—and it was paid for by the little guy. The little guy — you had zero on your savings account, you've got pension funds that have never had a bigger gap of returns, you can't do public bonds anymore because there's not enough yield. So it's the little guy — of every race, nationality, creed, ethnicity, gender, and sexual preference in the United States — the working class and the lower middle class, whose burden this became.

When people talk about anger, I think it's a kind of recognition that a certain group has done extraordinarily well — the greatest run we've had in owners of assets, whether intellectual property, stocks, or whatever, has been in the last ten or twelve years, because we have basically created money and floated our way out of here — and we haven't seen a "spread of the wealth," what I call a "piece of the action," given to the little guy.

So I think that was the beginning of populism. I think it's now tying up with what we call "economic nationalism," or just "nationalism" — this sovereignty movement. People saying, "Hey, I understand these international organizations, but I want my own nation to have its own sovereign role in the world."

RUDYARD GRIFFITHS: Give us a couple key planks of your populist platform, because ultimately populism is about the will of the people — what the people want — and therefore, I assume, what you believe the people need. So what is it? What's the Steve Bannon argument?

STEPHEN BANNON: Well, today we had a jobs report that shows a huge increase in manufacturing jobs in the United States, more increase in employment, and wages starting to rise. So, number one, populism is based around economics. It is basically about getting manufacturing jobs and high-valued-added jobs back to people in the United States. This is, kind of, the entire Trump economic program, and you're starting to see this. So I think the first plank is economics.

Number two is: we don't want interventions everywhere in the world — you're seeing this today as the United States is trying to get out of Yemen. We want allies. We're going to play an active part when it's in the vital interest of American national security, whether that's in Europe, the Persian Gulf, the South China Sea, or the Northwest Pacific; we're going to be there. But we're going to be there with allies, not with this kind of expeditionary tendency of the United States to try to spread democracy throughout the world. Our feeling, as populists, is that if democracy is going to spread, people in those countries have to want it, and have to work for it themselves. That's the second plank.

And the third is this huge Leviathan of the state, which really keeps the little guy down, and really emphasizes "crony capitalism"—a kind of "uni-party" permanent political class in Washington. The third plank is, how do you break that up?

Those are the three basic planks—anti-elite, anti-permanent political class, anti-consolidation of media and technology companies—of populism in the United States.

RUDYARD GRIFFITHS: Let me present you with a couple arguments you've no doubt heard before, and that I'm sure will be part of this debate, in terms of why populism *isn't* going to own the political future of the West. The first really revolves around the idea that the history of populist movements, in terms of their longevity, is not great. Often they burn themselves out—

STEPHEN BANNON: Or the Gracchi get murdered in Rome and thrown into the Tiber. It ends in tears.

RUDYARD GRIFFITHS: Exactly. The public is exhausted by it. They look for a unifier. They move on. And whatever populist movements or leaders there were are relegated to the dustbin of history. Why do you think this time is different?

STEPHEN BANNON: I think this time is different because of social media. I think people know they have to be engaged in the world or they're going to lose the sovereignty of their countries and they're going to lose any benefit to themselves. I think people understand now that this is a continual political process—it's not about any one election. And this is both on the left and the right. Remember, you have a strong "left-wing populism," and I think you're seeing that play out in this 2018 midterm campaign. I think people are energized, people are enthusiastic, and social media has gotten them to the ramparts.

You are absolutely correct: populist movements have died out in the past as things have gotten economically better. People have said, "Hey, maybe the elites aren't so bad. They gave me a taste, and I can live with that."

I think this time people realize you need more fundamental change. We're only at the top of the first inning, and here's one of the reasons: I think millennials are one of the biggest sources of populists we have out there. And the reason is they're like eighteenth-century Russian serfs. They're better fed, they're better clothed, they're in better shape, they're better educated, they have more information about the world — but they don't own anything. And they're not *going* to own anything. The way that we got ourselves out of the recent economic crisis was to make debt more achievable. In the United States, millennials have got $1.5 trillion of student debt; they've got consumer debt; they're 20 or 25 percent behind where their parents were at this age; and they're facing a housing crisis driven by this asset increase, which means they can't get a place to live. So right now — no ownership, the gig economy... I think millennials are the next big pool of populists, and that's one of the things we're really focused on.

RUDYARD GRIFFITHS: Your critics who are watching right now are saying to themselves, "God, this sounds reasonable; this almost sounds progressive." But they're also thinking about what they've seen in the United States since the election of President Trump—a surge in political violence on both sides.

STEPHEN BANNON: I don't know if that's true. I think that's just what the media is covering. And by the way, Antifa, and certain elements of Black Lives Matter, are just as bad as the Neo-Confederates. But both groups are small.

RUDYARD GRIFFITHS: But would you acknowledge that groups have tracked the rise of white supremacist violence in America, which *has* been up significantly over the last number of years? Where is that coming from? Are you saying that there's no connection between this populist surge and the spike in white supremacist terror?

STEPHEN BANNON: Absolutely not. The populist movement has nothing to do with white supremacy; it has nothing to do with that type of anger. People are angry, don't get me wrong, but I think they're angry with the simple fact that we've had an economic situation here where the elites took care of themselves, mitigated their own risks, and took all the upside.

Remember, two-thirds of our jobs are only at living wages or below. The average American family—I think it's 50 percent of our families—only have $400 in cash; the average net worth of an individual in the United

States, excluding their house, is something like $10,000. That's where the economic angst, the economic anxiety, and I think the anger comes from. I'm not saying there aren't fringe groups on both sides that are trying to start trouble, but I think the media overemphasizes it.

RUDYARD GRIFFITHS: Does it worry you when the president in the lead-up to the closing days of this midterm campaign has been out there aggressively portraying migrants—who look like a pretty harmless bunch, this so-called caravan—as terrorists and murderers? Are you worried that this rhetoric could incite people to violence toward disadvantaged communities?

STEPHEN BANNON: Here's what I'm worried about: the migrant crisis is a human tragedy of biblical proportions, but the solution is not going to be migrants coming up with the drug cartels, or now in human trafficking, and bringing people to the American border. The solution is not to put it on the backs of working-class people in Texas, New Mexico, and Arizona.

The president has his own house style, but I don't think he's inciting violence; I just don't. I do agree that he's been very forceful on this, and sometimes maybe he doesn't tie in the economic argument with it on the flip side. Sometimes he does, sometimes he doesn't. But I don't agree that he's inciting violence. I understand that that's the theme of the day: if you put CNN on, the top fifty stories are that. I just don't believe it, and I don't think Trump's base believes it.

RUDYARD GRIFFITHS: Another argument you're going to hear from your opponent tonight is that populism as it's manifested today has not undertones, but overtones, of corruption — at least in the examples of Russia, the Philippines, and non-first-world countries — and outright kleptocracy. Why are you confident that the populist movements in the West aren't similarly aligned to a lot of different elite interests? You could point to the tax cuts in the United States that advantaged the one percent; that's hardly advantaging the very folks that the movement was supposed to be helping.

STEPHEN BANNON: I think President Trump talked this week about more of a middle-class tax act. I was the guy in the Oval Office, as reported by the *Wall Street Journal* and others, who fought for a 44 percent tax on people who earn over $5 million. I thought that there were certain aspects also that could be much more populist.

The beating heart of it though — this corporate tax cut — was to bring manufacturing jobs back, which I think is the centrepiece of populism. It was not perfect, and as President Trump showed with his proposed middle-class tax cut, that's going to be a process.

Populists are not authoritarian, and certainly not totalitarian. The situations you talked about — Rodrigo Duterte and the kleptocracy in Russia — are more authoritarian models, and I don't think that's our model at all.

I also think you couldn't get more corrupt, more avaricious, than the permanent political class in Washington, D.C. The corruption in Washington goes through all bounds, and that has been a basic tenet of this populist movement since the Tea Party uprising in 2009 and 2010.

The problem we have today is when people say, "Oh, you guys are fascist." We're actually anti-fascist. Fascism worships the state and wants state capitalism to merge with the overweening state. We want to break that up. One of the basic tenets of this is that companies are too big and too powerful: the tech companies, the pharmaceutical companies, the media companies. This consolidation has made them too powerful with a compliant government, and that's where crony capitalism comes from, and that's where corruption comes from.

When you look at other countries, such as Italy, where crony capitalism exists — these big companies in bed with embedded governments with a *permanent* political class, where being a politician or a bureaucrat becomes a career — that's where you're seeing the populist movements. The Five Star Movement, or the League, are made up of people who aren't professionals. I don't want to call them amateurs, but they're just coming to politics as reformers. I think you're seeing the same thing here in the United States.

RUDYARD GRIFFITHS: One last argument that is often pushed back against populists is that the ideology that's going to win, or the movement that's going to win, is ultimately going to be the one that creates prosperity. How can you deny the prosperity that's been created through freer trade, open borders, and the free movement of people and ideas that has powered this *incredible* cycle of wealth creation, wealth generation, going back two or three generations? Why doesn't populism endanger all that?

STEPHEN BANNON: I don't think it does. I think what populists are saying is, "Hey, that worked out for the 'Party at Davos,' which took all the upside, financed off the back of the little guy, and protected in these national security relationships by the little guy." I think what they're saying is, "Hey, we're not trying to stop the wealth, and we're not trying to stop the prosperity." Look at the economic numbers that came out today: the manufacturing jobs, the lowest black unemployment in our history, the lowest unemployment since 1969. That's the heart of this economic nationalist, populist movement, and that's what we hope to spread. We're not trying to be isolationists from the world; we're not trying to be isolationists from trade.

Free trade is a *radical* idea, particularly when you have a totalitarian mercantilist society like China that you're competing with. So I think that we are going to see much more economic nationalism. But I think the whole point is to rebuild the manufacturing and industrial base of the United States.

The other thing is getting your voters out and convincing them. We couldn't have had a better run under Donald Trump, yet, as you can see, we're in a real fight for the House of Representatives and the Senate. And people say, "Hey, with a 'normal' president, he would be at 90 percent popularity." I also say, with a "normal president," which we had, we wouldn't have this kind of economic growth. You've got to take both together.

I think populism thrives as you make people's lives better, as you make things fairer. I don't think the little guy is looking for more government intervention. They're not looking for a handout; they're not looking for a hand up. What they want is not to have a system where wealth and power is concentrated in so few hands. And I think when you start to distribute that better, you're going to have a much more robust and vibrant economy and society.

RUDYARD GRIFFITHS: Final question. You're a student of history. What is the moment that we're in right now? Is the analogue the 1780s and '90s? Is it the 1860s? Is it the 1960s? What is the historical analogue to understand this tumultuous, tense cultural moment?

STEPHEN BANNON: I'm a believer in generational history. They talk about "The Turnings." I think we're in the great "Fourth Turning" of American history — there's a book on that if you want to catch up on it. We had the Revolution, we had the Civil War, we had the Great Depression and World War II. A "turning" comes about every eighty to a hundred years, just the way generations are raised, et cetera. And I think we're in the great Fourth Turning. It's all to be decided. That's one of the reasons I'm so excited to be part of this movement today.

I disagree with the ideology of the Left, but I admire the fact that the Time's Up movement, the resistance, and Tom Steyer have been doing what the Tea Party did in 2010. They have been walking neighbourhoods, ringing doorbells, making human contact — which is still the gold standard in how you get a vote, not a TV commercial—and they have generated tremendous enthusiasm. We are going to see that the "low propensity" voters on the left are voting. It looks like they've turned out their vote. I hope that we defeat that in a very close election on November 6.

But I think over the next ten, fifteen, or twenty years—at the ballot box and in the culture—we're not going to hug this out. We're going to fight it out. But we're going to fight it out politically, and not in the streets with all these groups that advocate violence and terrorism. We're going to do it the way it should be done: at the ballot box. And I think this November 6 could not be more exciting, because I think it's going to come down as a cliffhanger. And like I said: if they win it's because they outworked us. I'm a big believer in human agency, and I think that they will have just outworked us and outhustled us.

DAVID FRUM IN CONVERSATION WITH RUDYARD GRIFFITHS

❋

RUDYARD GRIFFITHS: David, thank you for coming to Toronto for this important debate. Let's start by having you define some terms so that people understand the context within which this debate is happening. You're going to argue in favour of small-*l* liberal values. Can you explain to me what those are for you, because I think there's a confusion out there: people hear "liberal" and they think capital-*l*, they think of a political party; they don't think of a kind of canon of foundational values.

DAVID FRUM: We have a vocabulary problem in modern politics. I'm a conservative, most of the time. But what do conservatives seek to conserve? What is the thing we inherited from the past that we are trying to protect? We're not trying to conserve the Spanish Inquisition;

we're not trying to conserve Versailles, an absolute monarchy; we're not trying to conserve Neanderthal cave art, attractive as it is. What we're trying to conserve is the liberal inheritance of the past two hundred years: the idea of the equal worth of the individual; the idea that the state should be the representative of the people, that those who hold power are accountable to those who confer power. We are trying to conserve the rule of law, limited government, market economics, and free trade as well. And we are especially trying to conserve a bunch of institutions that were created after World War II to make sure that the world would never undergo a catastrophe like that again — institutions that were supposed to mediate the differences between nations, and make sure that the zone of peace and like-mindedness was growing ever bigger.

RUDYARD GRIFFITHS: How is the outbreak of populism—not just here in North America, but now increasingly around the world—a threat to those small-*l* liberal values?

DAVID FRUM: Well, "populism" is an even more troubling word than "liberalism," and it has meant many more different things in many more different places. We use it mostly as a courtesy, because the people who espouse this politics, that's what they tend to call themselves. And that makes sense; I mean, who could be against populism, an idea that speaks for the people? But in democracy, populism always begins by taking a group of people and subdividing them, saying, "This group of people, because of their skin, because of their religion, because of some other factor:

they're not who we mean by 'the people.'" The foundation of this politics is a subdivision of the nation between the people who belong and the people who do not belong.

Now, this idea has also got a history. Because we live in a gentler world than our parents and grandparents did — although you can see a lot of family resemblance to the fascism of the 1930s and '40s in the populism of today — it's much less violent, it's much less dangerous, much less virulent. And so, as a courtesy, we use the term that the people use for themselves.

RUDYARD GRIFFITHS: So the alternative might be "authoritarian" or "fascist"? There's this word "nationalist." Your opponent tonight likes to call himself an "economic nationalist." How would you define that?

DAVID FRUM: Again, I'm not sure what that term means. "Nationalism" can mean a couple of things. One meaning suggests that you can enhance the economic well-being of a nation by sealing it off from trade, though I would just call that "uninformed." That's an intellectual error. You cannot do that. Nations that have tried it are poor; they're not pursuing welfare. But if what it means is that you envision a world of states in which the interests of states are in conflict, and that the project of harmonizing interests from nation state to nation state is a fool's errand, and that the truth is that nations compete aggressively against one another both in the sphere of economics and in other spheres, then I say let us be mindful of where this idea leads. Because it is just not true that you can see the world of commerce as competitive—as an area in which one nation's advantage comes at the expense of another's—and limit that view only to commerce. Sooner or later, this puts you on the path not just to trade war but to real war.

RUDYARD GRIFFITHS: You have written powerfully in your latest book, *Trumpocracy*, about how this new moment of populism has a kleptocratic "overture," that there's something new about how it's manifesting itself early on in the twenty-first century.

DAVID FRUM: Well, outside the Islamic world, the twenty-first century is not an age of strong ideology. We do not have the kind of demented idealism that you saw in the time of Stalin and Mao and Castro and Hitler. The modern authoritarians don't have big ideas. And again and again you see: they're in it to steal. That's one of the things that these nationalist heroes all have in common: they're all crooks. Viktor Orbán is plundering Hungary on a post-Soviet scale; the National Rally in France finances itself by a combination of dirty loans from Russia and fraudulently using its European Union parliamentary accounts; and the new government of Italy is caught up in a giant fundraising scandal. And, of course, Trump himself is the least ethical, least honest president in American history—and not just him but his cabinet are enmired in conflicts of interests. So populism also becomes a tool: you rev up not only people's hatred against others but their loyalty to you, and that enables you to steal from them and leaves them defenceless even to notice what's happening.

RUDYARD GRIFFITHS: Let me try out on you a couple of the arguments that surround this debate. The first is that politics has fundamentally changed — that in this age of exploding economic inequality, the axis of politics is the elite versus the people. It's no longer right versus left; it's no longer different interpretations of the liberal canon. Do you accept that politics has changed this way, and that this tendency will only get worse?

DAVID FRUM: Politics always changes. Politics is the art of governing human beings, and the questions are never the same; the challenges are never the same. And that's especially true in an era of rapid technological change. What I certainly do agree with is that the inherited arguments of left versus right from a previous era *have* become out of date, because they are arguments about things that people don't worry about so much anymore. And I would argue as well that extreme inequality does create challenges to the liberal order because it means that there are people who have power that in a liberal state nobody should have.

When I was studying Roman history as a boy there was this famous line from one of the Roman oligarchs who said, "No one should be considered rich unless he can afford to field a private army." In 1972 that seemed like a pretty laughable idea, but in 2018? Mark Zuckerberg could afford to field a private army; lots of people can afford to do that. We do live in a world of oligarchs. We live in a world of individuals who are as powerful as states. That's not a brand-new challenge. That's a problem that liberalism had at the beginning, back in the eighteenth century, when it had to confront these extraordinarily powerful monarchs and aristocrats who were stronger than the rest of the society put together. How do you apply the rule of law to such people? It's a real problem. But it's not a brand-new problem, and it's not a problem that invalidates the approach: we have to treat people with dignity and we have to have a state that answers to the government.

RUDYARD GRIFFITHS: Stephen Bannon argues vociferously that the liberal elite order has lost its political base, that it either ignored, or just didn't choose to care about, the hollowing out of the industrial heartland. It went off and fought a series of wars that cost trillions of dollars, and tens of thousands hurt and injured at home. In effect, the debate's over, because the liberal order can no longer recreate an electorate that's going to support these ideas because it squandered its own political capital.

DAVID FRUM: That is an assessment with a lot of validity to it. That's a true *observation*. It's not a true *recommendation*. As I will say tonight, Stephen Bannon and I have met once before. We met a decade ago; I was a participant in a film of his, and we discussed just this topic. I was writing a lot about this even before the 2008 financial crisis — that conservative politics had drifted away from the interests of the country. And Bannon saw it too, and we both realized that conservative politics as we'd known it had become obsolete. Now the question is, once you see that, what do you do? Do you try to reform, or do you take advantage of that fragility to overthrow — or to try to overthrow — a system?

So it's quite right that across the democratic world we have seen that the order built since 1945 has lost some of its popularity and legitimacy. And there are reasons why that's so. So let's correct the reasons. The alternative is not passive. The alternative is that people are saying, "Right; there's a loss of popularity here." That's an opportunity for somebody to do something very dangerous.

RUDYARD GRIFFITHS: And do you at this moment see the people who are exploiting that opportunity as responsible for this uptick in political violence, the increase of incidences of white supremacist terror in different Western countries around the world? Is it right to correlate those two?

DAVID FRUM: I want to be very precise in how I answer this. We can look at specific incidents. I think it is fair to hold President Trump very much to account for this pipe-bombing incident. The pipe bomber was someone who had been non-political before Donald Trump came on the scene, was politicized by Donald Trump, was an enormous enthusiast for Donald Trump, and chose his targets precisely according to the list that Donald Trump had given out. The people Donald Trump identified as his enemies became the pipe bomber's enemies, and he tried more or less wholeheartedly to murder them. I think Donald Trump needs to examine his conscience about all of that.

I don't think we do generally live in a time of increasing violence. I think that one of the things that characterizes our time is that, across the board, we live in a much less violent age than people did twenty, thirty, forty, fifty years ago. That's one of the reasons why people are tempted by this new kind of so-called populist politics. The people who experienced the high-octane version of this kind of politics back in the '30s and '40s knew how deadly it was. It led to murder; it led to war; it led to conflict; it led to cities that were eighteen inches high. And they said, "We will never, ever, taste this poison again."

But time passes and people forget, and then you get a milder version of the same thing and it doesn't look as violent. And in fact, many of its advocates would insist, "Well, we're not violent, we just want to have a *little* of the old poison."

RUDYARD GRIFFITHS: Where does this debate go from here? You're arguing tonight that Western politics can indeed have a liberal future. What makes you optimistic about that? Do you think it's a question of liberal internationalism becoming more effective, repositioning itself? Is it a case of populism burning itself out? What makes you hopeful about the future?

DAVID FRUM: The populists have no solutions. They don't care to have solutions. They don't even understand what a solution would look like. You take the two things that made Donald Trump, that were his hardest themes — economic conflict with China and immigration — and you know what? In 2018, Donald Trump will run a bigger trade deficit, with China specifically, than the United States has run in a decade. He doesn't understand the tariffs he applied. Any Econ 101 student could have told him that when the United States applies a lot of tariffs on China, what happens is that the U.S. dollar goes up and the Chinese currency goes down. And China's competitiveness is *enhanced* by the very things you try to do to punish China: bigger deficit. In the same way, President Trump ran very hard on the issue of immigration. Well, guess what? In 2018, illegal immigration will run *faster* than it did in the last two years of the Obama presidency. It's the same thing. Donald Trump can brutalize people, and insult and abuse them, but he doesn't have answers. So I think that's the first vulnerability of populist politics.

The second is that it is so corrupt, and so *flagrantly* corrupt. And people will — not the core constituents — but people will see it. Donald Trump is the least ethical president ever, and that offends people. And his cabinet is the least ethical cabinet in a long time. And people will see that. And they see the corruption as it happens with the little Trumps across Europe. There's a saying: "It's good to learn from experience; it's better to learn from other people's experience." But this may be one where we have to taste a little of this to remind ourselves why our parents and grandparents said, "Please, never again."

RUDYARD GRIFFITHS: So, just finally then — the future of these small-*l* liberal values: Do you think they are going to change? Do you think there's a need to look at greater redistribution of wealth, policies that are more focused on fairer trade as opposed to laissez-faire trade? Is there a recalibration that has to happen there too?

DAVID FRUM: Anybody who thinks that politics is going to the library, pulling a volume of Friedrich Hayek or John Maynard Keynes and searching through the index for answers to the questions they never thought of one hundred years ago … That's not how it works. What these traditions do is give you ways of thinking, and they give you values and guidelines.

We've now got this extraordinary accumulation of private wealth. That *does* challenge the liberal project. And it's not obvious what to do about it because the answers that a socialist would have, or that a communist would have, or that an authentic fascist would have are not available.

And in some countries — and this is especially true in Europe — the problem is that you have very sluggish local economies that don't create enough jobs. So it's true that in France what you need to do is a lot of deregulation to create employment and opportunity and get the economy moving, while in the United States you may need a thicker social insurance network to assure people that if, through no fault of their own, they get sick or lose their job or get old, they have less to fear.

We are going to have to think about how world trade works with the rise of China. It was always true in the past that the established trading powers were so rich and so strong that they could say to any newcomer, "Here are the rules you must obey." When you get a newcomer that is as big and powerful as China, you can't so easily tell them what the rules are; they have opinions of their own and they command a lot of authority.

The liberal tradition of the twenty-first century is going to have to be rethought. And so this democratic recession that we've had since 2005 — this may be the period in which we do the rethinking. What I hope is that our children and our grandchildren look back and say, "That was a dangerous period, and you all nearly made some very fatal mistakes, but you acted in time, you saw the danger, you corrected your own mistakes, and you reaffirmed the great tradition that has served peace and prosperity so well."

RUDYARD GRIFFITHS: You may have already answered my question, but what do you want—or what do you hope comes—out of this debate? There's been a lot of contention, a lot of debate *around* the debate. You were really committed at the very beginning to the idea of us talking about this, to having this conversation, as difficult as it was going to be. Why?

DAVID FRUM: I will open tonight's debate by answering just that question. But to anticipate a little bit, I have different answers for different people. Maybe the most important thing is: the people on my side of this argument—we've been losing, and we've been losing for a while. And since 2014, it's been one retreat after another, including in the very heartland of the country we look to defend and uphold: the United States. I think there's a lot of anxiety, a lot of discouragement, and some defeatism. And what I want to say tonight is, *Be not afraid.* It is true that things have been going ill. They are going to begin to go better. It is not too late; you can act. If you act now, you can turn this dynamic around, you can change this reality. The world is full of thugs and bullies and crooks who claim to be the wave of the future. They were wrong in 1942. They're wrong now.

The Rise of Populism

Pro: Stephen K. Bannon
Con: David Frum

November 2, 2018
Toronto, Ontario

RUDYARD GRIFFITHS: Good evening, ladies and gentlemen. Thank you for being here for the Munk Debate on the Rise of Populism. My name is Rudyard Griffiths and it's my privilege to organize this debate series and to once again to act as your moderator. I want to start tonight's proceedings by welcoming the North American–wide television and radio audience tuning in to this debate, everywhere from CPAC, Canada's public affairs channel, to C-SPAN across the continental United States, to CBC Radio's Ideas. A warm hello also to our online audience watching this debate right now via our social media partner, Facebook, on Facebook Live, and on the Munk Debate website. And finally, hello to you, the over 2,800 people and counting — who braved some protests tonight to be here in this hall for this important debate on this vital subject. All of us at the Munk Debates thank you for standing up for substantive, serious conversation on the big issues changing our world. Thank you. Bravo.

Thank you also to the Aurea Foundation, which has had the courage to support this series year in and year out for over a decade. Let's have a warm round of applause for the Munk family and the late, and great, Peter Munk.

Tonight's debate is happening just days before the critical midterm elections in the United States, and it will tackle one of the most important issues facing the Western world: the rise of populist politics. Tonight, we're going to ask these two debaters to answer some important questions. Is the West living through a populist sea change that will irrevocably transform our politics? Or can the long-standing liberal values — liberal values of trade, of society, of politics — push back against the populist surge and reassert their primacy in the twenty-first century? Let's find out by getting this debate underway, and getting our debaters out here centre stage.

Arguing in favour of tonight's resolution, "Be it resolved: the future of Western politics is populist not liberal," is the former strategist to President Donald Trump and global populist campaigner Stephen K. Bannon.

Speaking against tonight's motion is the bestselling author, the *Atlantic* magazine's senior editor, and staunch critic of President Trump and populist politics, Toronto's own David Frum.

For those of you watching online, we have a rolling poll and hashtag going tonight. That hashtag — and it's trending already, trust me — is #MunkDebate. You can also go onto our website, www.munkdebates.com/vote, and be part of a rolling poll that will assess these debaters' performance.

Finally, we have our countdown clock — and debaters pay attention, because this is important. In the final minute or so of each of the different segments of this debate, this audience will see a clock appear on the screen. When that clock reaches zero, join me in a loud round of applause, and that will keep our debaters on their toes, and our debate on time.

Now, this is going to be fun. Tonight, we're going to experiment with some live voting on the resolution. All of you received a clicker when you came in. Please take it out now and we're going to ask you to vote on the resolution.

If you are in favour of the motion, "Be it resolved: the future of Western politics is populist not liberal," I want you to press *A* or the number one on your clicker. If you are opposed to the motion, you're going to press *B* or the number two.

I'm going to remind the online audience that they can go to our website, www.munkdebates.com/vote. We've got a question live there right now that lets you vote on the resolution and also see how your fellow online watchers are gauging opinion at the start of this debate.

Okay, let's close that question now that we've all had a chance to vote, and let's see the results. What is this audience thinking as it goes into tonight's debate? How is public opinion divided in this room? There we have it: 28 percent of you agree with the resolution; 72 percent of you disagree. An interesting start.

Now we're going to ask a second question: Are you likely to change your opinion over the course of this debate? Might you hear something on stage that could cause you to switch your vote at the end of the evening? If you think you could change your vote, press the number one or the letter *A*. If your mind is set—if you're fixed here; if you're coming in with a view and you don't think you're going to get budged from it—press number two or the letter *B*. And again, to our online audience, you can do the same thing via our online poll.

Let's get those results up now. We're going to close that question and show our debaters how much opinion in this hall is in play—57 percent of you. A majority could potentially change their vote. So this debate is very much in play. Let's get it under way.

We're going to start with opening statements: eight minutes each—a bit longer than usual to give these two debaters time to articulate their views. And as per convention, the person speaking in favour of the motion will go first. So Stephen Bannon, I hand the podium over to you.

STEPHEN BANNON: Thank you. I want to thank the people of Toronto, and the Munk family, for hosting this and having me here tonight; and the men and women outside who are exercising their freedom-of-speech rights to protest.

It's not a question of whether populism is on the rise and going to be the political future. The only question before us is: Is it going to be populist nationalism or populist socialism? To understand the velocity, the intensity, the depth of the populist revolt on a global basis, we have to go back to the beginning, to what Hollywood would call the "inciting incident." I want to take you back to September 18, 2008, Washington, D.C., the Oval Office. I think it's ten or eleven o'clock in the morning, President Bush —

[shouts from the audience]

RUDYARD GRIFFITHS: We respect your right to free speech, but we have 2,800 people in this audience who want this debate to go on. Could I get a round of applause, please, for this debate to proceed? Thank you.

We're going to follow a policy tonight: this person has been cautioned. If she does not stop, she will be asked to leave this debate. Madam, it is your decision: you can stay or you can go. What are we going to do?

Okay, sorry; you're still engaging. Officers, we're going to move forward with our plan. If we can remove the person from the hall, please. Thank you very much. A big round of applause for the Toronto Police Service this evening — fabulous job. Okay, Stephen, you've got the floor again.

STEPHEN BANNON: Thank you. We're in the Oval Office. Head of the Federal Reserve Ben Bernanke and Secretary of the Treasury Hank Paulson walk in and tell the president of the United States, "By five o'clock this afternoon — by close of business — we need a $1 trillion cash infusion into the American financial system. If we don't get it, the American financial system will implode in seventy-two hours, the world financial system three days after that, and we will have global anarchy and chaos."

The greatest enemies to the United States—Mussolini, Hitler, Tojo, the Soviet Union, al-Qaeda, Osama bin Laden—nobody's ever brought the United States to its knees like that day. Who did that? Who's responsible for that? The populists? Donald Trump? No. The elites: the financial, the corporate, the permanent political class that runs Washington, D.C. That's who did it.

What was their solution? To create money and bail themselves out. On the day that happened, the balance sheet of the Federal Reserve was $880 billion. When Donald Trump took the oath of office on January 20, 2017, it was $4.5 trillion. We flooded the zone with liquidity, just like the Bank of Tokyo, the Bank of England, the European Central Bank. The "Party at Davos"—the elites—bailed themselves out, afraid of some sort of deflationary death spiral. That's not a free bailout; there's a corollary to that. Savings accounts are zero; pension funds have the biggest gap in history; you can't underwrite a bond in the United States because you only get—for a public school or waterworks—you get 2 percent. The little guy would bear the burden of that. If you've owned assets, intellectual property, stocks, real estate, hedge funds—you name it—in the last ten years, you had the greatest run in history. For everybody else, it was a disaster.

Fifty percent of American families can't put their hands on $400 in cash. Sixty percent of our jobs are subsistence jobs. The populist movement, the nationalist movement, is not a cause of that; it's a product of that.

Donald Trump's presidency is not a cause of that; it's a product of that. When I stepped into the campaign in mid-August, the central number was that 70 percent of the American people believed for the first time in our history that the country was in decline, and that the elites were okay with that. That "managed decline" was the wave of the future, whether it was education, the southern border, China, Korea, Iran, or our health system. It was Donald Trump who turned that around.

The "Party at Davos" — the scientific, managerial, engineering, financial, cultural elite who run the world — have left a financial wasteland, and have decoupled from the middle class and the working class throughout the world. That is why we have Matteo Salvini and Viktor Orbán, and Brexit, and now Jair Bolsonaro. It shouldn't be lost on you: the day Captain Bolsonaro is elected is the day Angela Merkel will leave the stage.

Trump's economic nationalism doesn't care about your race, your religion, your ethnicity, your colour —

[laughter from the audience]

Okay, okay; I've got a whole night to convert you — I saw the 28 percent!

It doesn't matter your gender, your sexual preference. Trump's economic nationalism only cares if you're a citizen. Look at the results: lowest black unemployment in history; lowest Hispanic unemployment in thirty years; wages rising across the board; manufacturing jobs coming back. The populist nationalist message and its policies are working in the United States. And it's spreading: the revolt in Europe and now in Latin America—and I get contacted every day from Asia, from Africa, from the Middle East. We're at the beginning of a new political revolution—and that is populism.

The only question before us is this: Is it going to be a populist nationalism that believes in capitalism, in deconstructing the administrative state, in giving the little guy a piece of the action, and in breaking up the "crony capitalism" of big corporations and big government? Or is it going to be a Jeremy Corbyn and Bernie Sanders type of populist socialism? Because the "Party at Davos" and the elites have blown too many calls—too many existential events: the rise of China; the $7 trillion spent on the wars in Iraq and Afghanistan; the deregulation that led to the financial crisis in 2008; the bailouts; where we are today in this overleveraged society—because as most of you in this room who work in finance know, we're heading toward another financial crisis.

That is the question before us. What form of populism? And I hope tonight that the good people in Toronto will listen with open ears as we debate this topic. Thank you very much.

RUDYARD GRIFFITHS: Thank you, Stephen. David, we're going to put eight minutes on the clock for your opening statement. You have the stage.

DAVID FRUM: Thank you. Well, I think we're all here to welcome Steve Bannon to President Trump's least favourite country. I worry that some of those protesters may have confirmed the idea that Canada does present a pillowcase national security threat.

I'd like to begin tonight by taking the protesters' question very seriously: "Why are we here and what are we hoping to achieve?" We're not here to mount an entertainment or to do a show. We are here to engage in the most important, most dangerous challenge that liberal democratic institutions have faced since the end of communism. Steve Bannon is a figure from history, a very important person. He advised the president of the United States at a time when that future president was on his way to losing, and Steve Bannon helped to turn the campaign around. He has been an advisor to parties all across Europe, many of which hold power, as in Italy. He has been an advisor to the new president of Brazil. His Breitbart.com became an *urgent* force in American politics, transforming conservatism into a new kind of political movement. All of that is his work.

So what do I hope to accomplish tonight by being here with him and engaging with him? I want to do three things.

First, I want to speak to those who are genuinely undecided. There may not be so many, but you are important. And you may be wondering, "Does the kind of politics Steve Bannon is speaking for, and that President Trump articulates, does that politics offer me anything? Should I listen to it?" I'm here tonight to tell you, it offers you *nothing*. It does not care about you; it does not respect you. Steve Bannon has said, in an interview with Michael

Lewis in February, "It is anger and fear that drives people to the polls." Anger and fear is what is offered, but nothing substantial.

Second, in addition to those who are undecided, I want to speak to those of you who see President Trump's politics for what it is, and who resist it. I know how worried you are, I know the fear that many feel, and I stand here to reignite your faith and to speak to your courage. These symbols that many of us wear tonight on our lapels [*points to Remembrance Day poppy pin*] remind us that this is not the first time that democracy has faced thugs and crooks and bullies and would-be dictators, and those who seek to build themselves up by tearing others down. This is not the first time such people have puffed themselves as the wave of the future. They were wrong then; they are wrong now. We are here to show that we are what our parents and our grandparents were. And the challenges and threats they met and overcame — we can do the same.

The last group of people I want to speak to — and maybe this is the most important — are those who see Trump's politics for what it is, and who support it anyway. Many people are excited by the joy of destruction, wrecking things they could never build, smashing things they do not understand. Steve Bannon has talked of "burning everything down." I'm sure he means that metaphorically. But we are nearing the eightieth anniversary of Kristallnacht, and there are people who understand burning non-metaphorically, and I'm here tonight to speak to all of them and to say, "You will lose; you will lose. You have been winning" — it has been five good years for those people—"but you will lose. And when you lose, your children will be ashamed of you, and they will disavow you, and the future will not belong to you. And it starts tonight."

Now, we have a definitional problem as we begin this debate because we're using words that have large meanings—"liberal," "populist"—and we're not exactly sure how to use them. And many people have made the point that it's strange for me, a lifelong conservative, to be here on the "liberal" side of this debate; I am not a liberal. I am a conservative, but what I and other conservatives in the English-speaking world have historically sought to conserve is a "liberal heritage," and this is something that conservatives and liberals share. We are trying to conserve a state that does not steal, a media that does not lie, courts that respect the rights of all, and voting that is available to everybody, even if the people who are counting the votes are afraid that those who are voting may vote against them.

And what is populism? It claims to speak for the people, but it always begins by *subdividing* the people and by saying *some* among the people—because of their skin, or the way they pray, or their gender, or whom they love, or how they conduct themselves, or for some other reason—*some* of the people are not *the* people, they are *those* people. Populism begins by dividing the country between *those* people and *us* people, and saying, *those* people do not matter and *our* people do. You can see President Trump doing this again and again, when he say things like, "I got 52 percent of the vote of women." Well, that's not true. He got 52 percent of the vote of *white* women, but the others don't matter. For him "the people" is always, *always*, only *part* of the people. Those who think differently, and those who report on our crooked business deals, or our clandestine connections with hostile foreign powers, they are *enemies* of the people, even though they are exercising the rights that you would think would belong to the people.

Why will this populist movement lose, and why will our liberal institutions prevail? At the bottom, it's for one reason: this new populism is a scam — it's a lie; it's a fake; it has nothing. I don't mean that just in the sense that so many of its leaders are crooks, although they are: President Trump is a crook; Viktor Orbán is a crook; Marine Le Pen is a crook. And I don't mean that in the sense that they say things that are not true — Viktor Orbán is looting Hungary on a post-Soviet scale, Marine Le Pen finances her party with Russian money and by stealing European parliamentary funds, and Donald Trump is running the most unethical administration in American history, enriching himself as he goes. I mean it in another way, because it is a scam even on its own terms. What do they deliver? Donald Trump is running the American economy the way he ran his family businesses: he inherited a fortune, has proceeded to dissipate it, and is telling everybody what a great job he's been doing. President Trump today took credit for the fact that in the month of October, 250,000 jobs were created in the United States. Congratulations, that's a good number. There were twenty-six months under President Obama where that many jobs were created, and there were five months under President Obama when 300,000 jobs were created. It's not Donald Trump's doing, no matter how much he says it is. But here's what *is* his doing: the biggest trade deficit with China since before the Great Recession, and illegal immigration that is running faster than it ran in the two years before he took office.

There's going to be a lot more to talk about tonight, but I want to just reassure all of you: liberal democracy is stronger than it looks. Since 1945, it has built the most decent, best societies ever seen, and the new populism is based on one assumption—

RUDYARD GRIFFITHS: Your time is up, I'm afraid. Ladies and gentlemen, we're going to do something a little different tonight: we're going to have timed rebuttals. We're going to let both of these debaters engage with what they've heard in the opening statements and really get this debate underway. We're going to have two of these rounds. Stephen, you're up first. We'll put three minutes on the clock for you.

STEPHEN BANNON: This is the oldest trick in the book— just smear the populist movement, smear the "deplorables." Hillary Clinton tried that. We saw how it turned out.

David, the reason that Donald Trump and the populist movement rose is because of the George W. Bush administration, which you worked in. You keep talking about the ability to make these decisions, and how great a decision you're making, and all these scumbags and thieves that are in the populist movement. The reason you don't like it today is liberal democracy. The concept in the *Economist* is *illiberal* democracy. The reason you call it that is, of course, Orbán is winning with 70 percent of the vote; Luigi Di Maio and Matteo Salvini are winning with two-thirds of the vote; Captain Bolsonaro wins with 55 percent of the vote; Donald Trump wins with over three hundred electoral votes.

During President Bush's watch, we saw the inexorable rise of China. It was said that it was the second law of thermodynamics: they were going to become a liberal democracy and a free-market capitalist society. And we just watched the beginning process of the deindustrialization of the United States, shipping all the manufacturing jobs over there. If you read J. D. Vance's *Hillbilly Elegy*, the great sociological study of the "deplorables," it shows a direct correlation between the factories that left, the jobs that went with them, and the opioid crisis. They took away people's self-worth and dignity. Then there was the "great decisions" and the $7 trillion — that's a Brown University Watson Institute figure, not Breitbart; that's their analysis of what it costs on these wars that we still haven't won and are still in, seventeen years later, with 10,000 dead, 40,000 or 50,000 combat casualties, and $7 trillion spent. And finally there's the financial debacle. On *their* watch.

It's easy to sit here with all these highfalutin terms and to say how "racist" the movement is. The populist movement is not racist. Look at the economic benefits that are coming through President Trump's policies. And if you believe for a second my opponent's thing about Obama — he didn't understand the math between $880 billion and

$4.5 trillion. It's pretty easy to create things when you're flooding the zone with capital and destroying the basics of the Judeo-Christian-West family, which is saving. You cannot save anymore; you don't have a pension plan. That is all the work of the "great elites," of the permanent political class, that look at the populists as a bunch of racist, nativist xenophobes. Well, they're not. They're the backbone of our country, the most decent people on earth. Here in Canada you're built upon the same building blocks of the little guy, for the common good.

DAVID FRUM: I did work for Present Bush, and I served him on one of the darkest days in American history, 9/11. I was in the White House that day, and I saw what the American spirit could be. Steve Bannon voted for President Bush twice—I believe that's correct?

And we have one other thing in common. He may not remember this, but this is actually the second time he and I have met. The first was when I made an appearance in one of his films. It was about ten years ago. I got a call from a friend of mine. There was this Wall Street banker who was setting up a new career as a Hollywood producer. Would I be interviewed for one of his movies? And we talked about these very themes. And at the end of it, Steve Bannon kindly sent me back to work in one of his limos. So I am very surprised to see my old producer-friend now emerging as this fiery tribune of populism.

It is absolutely true that liberal democracy is in trouble now because of the failures that have happened in the past, because of the financial crisis, and because of unsuccessful wars. And it is true that liberal democracy got into trouble in the 1930s because of mistakes that were made: there would have been no fascism had the 1920s led to permanent success. But the failures of a good system are not a reason to turn to an evil one. We have to renew and repair.

When Steve Bannon and I talk, one of the things we have in common — and this is one of the things I really credit him for — is that in a world of Republicans who said that everything was fine, Steve Bannon was one of the first people to say that things were not fine. We saw the same thing. We saw the stress that was happening to middle-class incomes, and we saw the tensions that were rising as wealth became more extremely unequal in the United States.

I think one of the reasons that it's interesting to reconnect after this time is because we had very different responses to that. The populist movement sees those fissures as opportunities to exploit, to destroy, and to overthrow; I see them as flaws that demand reform, constructive repair, and renewal.

What you're being asked to vote on tonight is not whether everything was handled well in the Bush years. During what period in history was everything handled well? The questions are: What are you going to do about it? How are you going to respond? What kind of world do you want to build? The choice is between destruction and renewal, between freedom and non-freedom. The choice is between a society that respects everybody — *all* the people — and a politics that defines the people against the people, that always excludes someone, and that makes the basis of the nation the suppression of much of the nation.

STEPHEN BANNON: David Frum needs no introduction; he's one of the most significant public intellectuals in the United States and the conservative movement. And, yes, I reached out to him when I made a film about the financial crisis because I needed his intelligence, I needed his perspective, I needed his wisdom. It's a very high priority for me and others in the populist movement to convert people like David Frum to our cause.

We're not trying to stop elections. We're going to win elections! We love elections, because we're going to win. Victory begets victory. We're not saying, "Don't have elections." We're the true anti-fascists: fascism looks to *worship* the state.

The Trump movement has three things: economic nationalism, an "America First" national security policy, and deconstruction of the administrative state. The progressives over the last forty or fifty years have built up an administrative state bigger than the cabinet departments. It's a fourth branch of government. That's why Neil Gorsuch and Brett Kavanaugh are in the Supreme Court— the Chevron exemption—they're all about deconstructing. It's not deregulation: it's about taking the Leviathan apart brick by brick, which David Frum has argued *for*, for thirty years of his professional life. Economic nationalism is putting your country first when it comes to the economy, and to not have the maximization of shareholder value but the maximization of *citizenship* value.

If the Trump program and the populists are so bad, David, how did we get the new NAFTA deal? And the key to the NAFTA deal is to create a geostrategic manufacturing base that will counter East Asia, and not allow China to game the system through Mexico. The benefits of this — as you see the supply chains, you see the European Union and Japan and Korea have bilateral deals with us — are going to be enormous. It's like the original NAFTA, when Canada's economy went up ten times because of the manufacturing it took from the United States. You're going to see the supply chain start to come back.

The rules-based international order rests on the back of the "deplorables"; it's their sons and daughters in the Hindu Kush, in the South China Sea, on the thirty-eighth parallel. That network of commercial relationships, capital markets, trade deals — from Europe, to the Persian Gulf, to the South China Sea, to the Northwest Pacific — President Trump is trying to reinforce that: make NATO work; make the Gulf Emirates work; have free navigation of the South China Sea.

DAVID FRUM: How did we get the new NAFTA? I'm going tell you a story — and this is a true story, ominously enough — about how President Trump found his most important trade advisor. When he, to his surprise, won the election of 2016, he decided trade with China was going to be an issue. So, as one does, he asked his son-in-law to find him a trade advisor. Jared Kushner, as one does, went to the Amazon website and typed the words "China" and "trade" into the browser, and he pulled up a video called *Death by China*, made by a man named Peter Navarro. It was a very exciting video—lots of flames. Peter Navarro does have a PhD in economics, but no peer-reviewed articles. I think he was teaching—I don't know where he was teaching—and he's now the chief trade advisor to the United States. And maybe it fits, because when President Trump was making notes on his approach to trade, as Bob Woodward reports, he wrote as a prompt in one of his speeches, "TRADE IS BAD."

So how did we get the new NAFTA? A lot of responsible people surrounded Donald Trump and tried to encourage him to do as little damage as possible to the most important trading zone on earth. And the good news is that, although the president crashed into the podium and knocked the cell phone to the floor, the screen was not too badly damaged. And NAFTA is waiting there to be repaired and brought into the modern age when there are people with good faith who can do things like negotiating the digital economy—none of which got done. *No* constructive work got done. All that happened was that NAFTA was prevented from being destroyed.

One of the issues we talk about here tonight is nationalism and globalism. "Globalism": it's supposed to be a bad word. North American lungs breathe Chinese pollution; Russian missiles shoot down Malaysian airliners with European citizens aboard. The only way we are going to stop this planet from getting too hot for our species to live on is if we all work together. It's one planet.

We love our countries. Only through countries can we exercise our democracy. But we work together with friends and partners. How did Donald Trump get NAFTA? By *bullying* people, not by treating them as partners. He's never been able to negotiate a win-win deal in his business career. Both Canada and Mexico are less powerful than the United States, and in the past America always said, even though that was true, "We can work co-operatively together." But this idea of America First, or Hungary First, or France First, or Germany First—it gets progressively less attractive, doesn't it, as we name the other countries who are going to put themselves first?—we left that behind to say, "We are going to build a community of democratic nations who understand that of course there are clashing interests that have to be worked out, but we are stronger, *always*, when we work co-operatively, and that we can build peace and prosperity." That's a liberal idea, in the truest sense, because the central thing we've been arguing about for two hundred years is: Is the relationship of human beings one of domination and oppression, or one of potential fruitful co-operation? And that's the question on the ballot tonight.

STEPHEN BANNON: As I've gone around and met the leaders of the populist nationalist movement in Europe— and I'm not an advisor to these individuals; I've set up a group called "The Movement" to be kind of, hopefully, the interconnective tissue that can help them focus on the European parliamentary elections next year—not one leader, haven't heard one say they want to destroy the European Union. What they talk about is the sovereignty of their country. They want their countries back, and they want their countries to be sovereign entities. And they want their citizens to be empowered, and not to report to these trans-national entities that have no accountability, the European Central Bank and the EU. They don't want to make the European Union the United States of Europe, where Italy's like South Carolina and France is Georgia; they want to make it a collection of sovereign individual states that work together.

Why is that so hard, and why is that demonized? Why is the nation state — that's been with us since the Treaty of Westphalia and is the central building block of our world — why is it all of a sudden so scorned? Why is the term "nationalism" so scorned and demonized? What people want is *subsidiary*: they want as much control as they can have *as citizens*, and that's through the nation sate.

Donald Trump gave that back to the American people. I know you may mock and ridicule it. But the economic turnaround didn't come from Obama, and everybody in the United States knows that. The most progressive president in the United States — and he can't defend this — flooded the zone and bailed out the elite in our country. We have socialism in the United States for the very wealthy and the very poor, and a brutal form of Darwinian capitalism for everybody else: the devil take the hindmost.

That's what the future entails if we don't get this right in Trump's administration and further administrations, if we don't bring out the benefits of capitalism. The millennials are nothing but eighteenth-century Russian serfs right now. They're better fed, they're better clothed, they're in better shape, they have access to more information, but they don't own anything and they're not going to own anything. Because of what Obama did, they're 20 percent behind where their parents were at the same age. And they live in a gig economy; they can't afford a house, there's no pension plans, there's no careers. That, by the way, is the biggest potential for our populist movement — the millennials — because they're going to see the logic of what we are talking about.

Once again, David, we are not saying we shouldn't have elections. You just don't like it now because the established Republicans can't win any elections.

DAVID FRUM: Oh my Lord, did they bring me to Toronto to defend the Obama economic record? This is a weird argument to be having at the end of the worst month in financial markets since the financial crisis of 2009. The financial markets are telling you the Trump economy is careening to disaster.

Steve Bannon cares a lot about manufacturing jobs. Since the bottom of the recession — I looked all these things up; I don't carry this around in my head — since the bottom of the recession, the United States economy has created 1.2 million manufacturing jobs. Two-thirds of those jobs were created while Barack Obama was president, one-third since Donald Trump has taken the presidency. The Trump economy is the *continuation* of the Obama economy, but with more tariffs, more inflation, and higher interest rates. And as Steve Bannon himself very astutely said, there is a giant financial crisis headed our way—but it's not created by Ben Bernanke; it's created by the actions of this presidency.

Populism always ends in economic disaster because populist economics is not interested in results, and it's not interested in the future. It is an attempt to exploit emotions to gain power. President Trump, on the campaign trail, kept accusing the Democrats of wanting to turn the United States into Venezuela. But it's his policies that are inspired by Juan Perón's Argentina: high tariffs, massive borrowing. The United States is going to run a trillion-dollar deficit in the coming fiscal year, a bigger deficit than George H. W. Bush ran to win the First Gulf War, and a bigger deficit than George W. Bush ran to fight the Second Gulf War. And all of this is coming to a head, and the financial markets are telling us this.

It is a funny thing to talk about millennials here—I don't know if there are very many here, unfortunately. A few? Some of mine? They're unpersuaded. They're unpersuaded; they're un-mobilized. Because like all people, millennials can feel when they are respected, and they know who has their interests at heart. And they are going to demonstrate on Tuesday who they feel is not protecting them.

But this debate involves them in another way, because what we're really arguing about is not who's right or wrong—although of course I'm right—but about to whom the future belongs. It's possible to be right and still to lose. The future belongs to my side of the argument because the future only belongs to those who care about it. The future does not belong to those who immolate the future in order to achieve a temporary advantage. That is the policy of the Trump administration, and that's what all of these high-inflation, high-tariff parties across Europe are. They don't know what they want to do; they only know who they hate. And hate doesn't build.

RUDYARD GRIFFITHS: I'm going to put another three minutes on the clock for you, Steve — you're not getting off easy tonight! Another three minutes. Come back on David on those points.

STEPHEN BANNON: You know this is the whole thing, the other smear, which I never thought David would stoop to, given my esteem for him as a public intellectual. This whole thing about hate. Donald Trump is supposed to hate Muslims, right? He's supposed to be an Islamophobe. Where's the first place Donald Trump went?

The Islamic world had reached out to us. There had been limited engagement during the Obama administration. The Obama administration was engaged with Iran, so the first summit in Riyadh was set up to talk about and discuss three things that they brought up: One, how do you eradicate Islamic terrorism from the face of the earth? By cutting off the financing; two, how does the Arab world come together as one with Israel, to stop the expansion of Iran?; and three, the Islamic world says, "We know we have to go through some sort of form of modernity; can you assist us in some way? We have to do this ourselves." Three things they wanted to discuss, even before we won the election, when Trump met with them at the UN.

So how does Trump get called a "hater"? He went over there and said, "Here's the system of how we stop the financing of radical Islamic terrorism, because it's blowing back on your societies today, and Western Europe and the United States." And look at the improvement we've made in just two years. Look at the eradication of the physical caliphate of ISIS that was done in conjunction. Remember, in 2014, ISIS had eight million people under slavery, they had oil wells, they were taxing people. That was Trump coming together with the Muslim world to destroy ISIS.

In addition, it was the beginning of an alliance, the beginning of a partnership — as imperfect as it is in that part of the world — with the Arab world, and Israel, and the United States, and the nations of Europe, to stop the expeditionary expansion of Hezbollah in Iran.

And the third was to assist the Arab world in any way — understanding that they have to do it, just like Christianity had to do it — to go through its own Enlightenment.

And yet Trump is smeared every day as an Islamophobe and a hater. He's anything but. It's his actions, his actions, his *actions*. Look, it's the signal in the noise. Listen to the signal. He puts it out every day through actions. The noise I understand is a flashbang grenade.

RUDYARD GRIFFITHS: You guys have been superb; you practically made me irrelevant in this debate, and that's a sign of a great debate — when the moderator doesn't have to step in. But I want to just cover off a couple of questions that I know are on people's minds watching online and in this audience.

David, I'm going to start with you and the midterms — a critical test for this presidency. Trump seems to have campaigned out of a populist playbook: hard message on immigration — some would say a *shocking* message on immigration — hard message on China and on trade, and a demonization of the media and so-called elites. Why isn't that a powerful proof point for your opponent here tonight: the effectiveness those populist memes seem to have with the American voter, as opposed to your liberal idealism?

DAVID FRUM: Well, we will see how powerful they are. But I think Donald Trump is president not just because of those notes but because of something else he did — and Steve Bannon was there, and this was very clever. Donald Trump campaigned in 2016 as the one Republican who would respect and protect Americans' health insurance. He gave an interview in September on *Dr. Oz* — that's a program that probably a lot of people in this room and the dreaded elites do not watch, but it's watched by a lot of people; 80 percent of his audience has a household income of less than $30,000 a year — and Donald Trump said on the program, "We're going to come up with plans, health care plans, that will be so good and so much less expensive, both for the country and for the people, and so much better." Lack of detail, but you hear the commitment.

So what did he do? Nothing. Health care under Donald Trump — especially for the *Dr. Oz* audience — is worse. His administration is in court right now trying to make it possible for insurance companies to deny coverage to people who are already ill. And the Democrats are talking about health insurance. Republicans should have had an answer to this question. One of the dreaded elites whom I quite like, Mitt Romney, he did — and he actually got a larger share of the popular vote than Donald Trump, but the ball didn't bounce right for him in the Electoral College, and so this job was left for Barack Obama to do. But that is going to be a pounding, because the people who we are supposedly here to protect, the people who — if we actually are concerned for them and are not just using them — need a health system that works for them, and Donald Trump has blown it up.

RUDYARD GRIFFITHS: Steve, we come to you on a midterm question also. You've said it: this is a critical test for your guy, this president. If he does not maintain both houses, his presidency is in real danger, according to *you*. That's the end of his populist movement; that's the end of your populist icon.

STEPHEN BANNON: We're just in the top of the first inning of populism. This is a critical test, there's no doubt about it. I believe we will hold the Senate, and I think it's a complete dogfight for the house, but we'll see. If we lose the House of Representatives, as I've told you — and I've seen David talking on TV — the Trump program will grind to a halt; there's no doubt about that.

But remember, we understand it's a process. Both Brexit and 2016 are inextricably linked. Look at Brexit two years later: they're no closer to a deal than when they first started because the establishment wasn't just going to pat the British workers on the head and say, "What a great idea! Why don't you just leave the EU?" Just like with Donald Trump, they're not going to pat him on the head and say, "This is fantastic — all your great populist and economic nationalist ideas — why don't you just take the keys and run for it?" You are going to have to win election after election after election, and I think the Trump base understands that. I anticipate it's going to turn out.

I want to address one thing with David. When we won as a coalition, one of the first things I did was reach out to the Republican establishment in mid-August. We had to win as a coalition, just like the Reagan coalition, where you had economic conservatives, and you had anti-communists, and you had the religious right. We have the same thing: we have the establishment, we have the populist nationalist movement, we have limited-government conservatives. We are a broad coalition; that's what needs to come together to win.

In governing, David, we turned immediately to the Republican Party, our partner in that victory, who said, "We've got it. Give us the keys on health care; we've been working on this for seven years." The entire debacle on health care in that first year was 100 percent the Republican establishment. It turns out they didn't really have an idea about health care.

The same thing with taxes. Remember, we were going to start with the "border adjustable" tax that Paul Ryan had worked on for seven years. In ninety days, that got blown up, and we had to do the tax plan we had. By the way, as many of you know who read the *Wall Street Journal*, I argued in the Oval Office for a 44 percent tax rate for people who make over $5 million a year, and I was blown up! I was blown up by the progressive Democrats in the administration, the Wall Street guys, who forced in the big tax cuts—which President Trump has now realized, I think, was not actually the best thing to do. That's why he brought the middle-class tax cut last week. It takes a while. He's getting his sea legs, you don't start day one…

RUDYARD GRIFFITHS: David, do you want to jump in? I think that's a great segue to bring some Frum into the conversation.

DAVID FRUM: The best defence of Donald Trump is: the job's just too hard for him. The best defence is that he looks cruel and unfeeling and bigoted and hateful, but really, the problem is that he's just never run a large enterprise before, and he's certainly never paid his debts before, so how could he do it? The buck must stop anywhere else.

Donald Trump did all these things; he signed all these things. It is an amazing fact about the presidency that you do have to deal with other people, and you do have to make compromises, and you do have to build coalitions. And if you can't do that, then you're not very good at the job of being president.

STEPHEN BANNON: The economy is not only growing at 3 percent, 3.5 percent, some say maybe 4 percent—I realize we owe President Obama all that—but Trump is taking liquidity out of the market. He's taken $360 billion in quantitative tightening; he has not opened up the spigots to liquidity.

And what's he doing to our national security—he is the one who's trying to *rejuvenate* NATO. He is the one who's sitting there going, "The British can put up one combat division, the French two combat divisions, all the rest of NATO a combat division. The United States can't bear the entire burden." We have a $1 trillion defence bill. I know it says $780 billion—it's a trillion dollars. We can't afford to continue to do that. It's not that we don't want to be engaged in the world—and we *will* be engaged in the world. But what Trump is saying, from Europe to the Persian Gulf, South China Sea, Northwest Europe: it's trade deals, commercial relationships, capital markets—and an American security guarantee. That has to change and we have to have partners, like we have allies in Canada, in Israel, in the United Arab Emirates; everybody else has to step up and be an ally. We're not looking for protectorates; that's what Trump's saying. I haven't seen—and, David, we can get into this, though I don't want our discussion of populism to devolve into one about Trump's presidency—I haven't seen a bad decision from Trump yet.

DAVID FRUM: When we talk about Trump and NATO, this is where I really feel for the poignancy of Steve Bannon's position tonight. Steve Bannon wore the uniform of the United States. I believe your daughter wears it now?

STEPHEN BANNON: Yeah, she's in the First Airborne.

DAVID FRUM: And Steve Bannon described the Trump family's meeting in Trump Tower with agents of the Russian state as borderline treason. So, I accept that you believe in America's defence relationship with its traditional allies. But your president does not, and his family does not, and they are *selling* the United States.

STEPHEN BANNON: Let's talk about NATO, because this is about America First national security. Donald Trump is trying to save that alliance. What he is saying is that people have to put in 2 percent of GDP; you just can't continue on like this. When we first stepped in, we put in a $30 billion supplemental, just because of operational readiness. The Italian and German defence budgets are not more than $30 billion. We're not looking for protectorates. And that's what Trump is saying. Trump is more engaged in the Persian Gulf, he's more engaged in the South China Sea, he's more engaged in the Northwest Pacific, he's more engaged in NATO than any president in living memory, but he's doing it in a way to say, "Hey, we can't bear the entire burden anymore, we just can't." The "deplorables"—it's all on their shoulders; it's their kids and their money. And it's come time that we're not looking to be an empire. We're not an *imperial* power, we're a *revolutionary* power.

DAVID FRUM: If the idea is—as you've suggested a couple of times—that it's the "deplorables," meaning Trump supporters, who are doing the fighting for the United States, this is an example of one of the real ills of populism, because, may I remind you, that force is one-third made up of non-white people who certainly did not vote for Donald Trump, and they get forgotten and omitted from the story. We have to be able, as we see the United States, to see it *as it is*. You're only a patriot if you love your country *as it is*, not as you imagine it might have been in the past, and not if you begin to chop off groups of people you think do not belong there.

Donald Trump made it clear through the campaign that if it's up to him, NATO countries are not being defended. He told Maggie Haberman and David Sanger of the *New York Times* in an interview at the time of the Republican convention that Estonia is not going to be defended if it's up to him. Estonia is a NATO partner.

But there's something else overhanging all of this. I don't think you can talk about the Trump foreign policy — or any of these parties that you advise through Europe — without acknowledging that they all have some sinister murky connection to Russian power. The National Rally: funded by them. Your Italians friends... And as I said, I do not put this on you — I know you wore the uniform. But I don't know how you, having worn the uniform, can sit with these people who have these sinister connections and know that there is someone else who does not have the interests of your country, my adopted country, at heart. And he is calling the tune for all of these populist parties.

from the things he says. I wrote words for a president, and one of the things I learned was that what a president says is what a president does. Now, obviously President Trump is in no way accountable for that terrible crime in Pittsburgh—obviously. What he *is* accountable for is what he didn't do decently afterwards—that he could not find words; he could not find something in himself. Now, that's a personal failing, and maybe it doesn't have political consequences. But the pipe bombs—that's a different story, because that person was someone who was previously completely un-political, who became political in 2016, became obsessed with Donald Trump. And every one of the people who got a pipe bomb was a *named* target of President Trump's.

Now, if somebody had listened to Eric Holder and had decided to take him literally rather than metaphorically—as he obviously intended—and somebody had gone on a kicking rampage, and kicked somebody to death, and it turned out he had Eric Holder posters all over his room, I bet we'd see a pretty contrite Eric Holder today. But that didn't happen. What *did* happen, though, was that pipe bombs went to the people President Trump had named and President Trump said, "I blame the people who got the pipe bombs!"

STEPHEN BANNON: David, you just said that President Trump made them targets. President Trump never made them targets. Maybe in speeches over time he singled those people out, but he's never sat there and said, "They're targets." You can't equate the two.

DAVID FRUM: There are 330 million people in the United States, and most of them, of course — like all people everywhere — are wonderful. But some are disturbed. The unconscious mind always seeks to be taken seriously, to express itself in terms that are intelligible. And presidents do set tone and give permission. Now, most of us will never behave wrongly no matter who the president is, and that's why American society is not dissolving as we speak — because if people acted like the president, the place would be Gotham City. But there are people who are at the cusp, and who are asking themselves, "Are my behaviours normal?"

We have seen that. And this is one of the reasons that Breitbart was so powerful — unfortunately, I think, not for good. You can see the *radicalization* that has happened even within the sort of so-called legitimate conservative media: how much more radical Fox News is; how much more credence it gives to crazy conspiracy theories; and how much more, by the way — while of course no one wants violence — how much more airtime it gives to subliminal, anti-Semitic messaging. I think every Jew who hears the way George Soros is talked about knows the text beneath the text. I can't, of course, put myself completely in other persons' shoes, but I try to imagine how it must sound to black people, or to Mexican-Americans, or to Asian-Americans, or to members of any other group. When you hear this barrage, and you hear something that seems like, "Oh, we're just talking about this *one* shadowy mastermind — this plutocratic person — who bends the world to his will through his monetary conspiracy; not everybody else, just this *one* person." We all hear it and we know what is meant, and it has resonance though history, and we feel endangered.

RUDYARD GRIFFITHS: Now, just so the audience knows where we're going, we'll have you respond to that, Stephen, and then we'll go to closing statements.

STEPHEN BANNON: We're having such a good time; I thought we could engage some more. Let's waive our closing statements and still have combat!

George Soros — I said it in the *New York Times* the other day — George Soros is demonized because he's *effective*, not because he's Jewish, and he's very proud of how effective he's been. I kind of model myself and my NGOs on George Soros — that's how effective he's been in Europe and the United States. And he has not been shy about bragging about that over the last ten years, about what he's done, how much money he's put to work. He's been incredibly effective. In that regard, he is a role model. But as I said the other day, when you're that "out there" — I've got security all the time and I'm a "grundoon" — it's the admissions price. When you're dealing in this type of environment, it's the admissions price. This is not about George Soros being Jewish.

It's just like "globalist"; it's not about the Illuminati, or the Jesuits, or the Freemasons, or the *Protocols of the Elders of Zion*. The "Party at Davos" — and this is the thing — it's no conspiracy; it's in your face! It's in your face every day. Look at the anonymous op-ed that was written about President Trump, this kind of rolling coup in his administration. They're quite proud of the establishment Republican who said, "We're the 'steady state.'" That's what it is. There's no hidden conspiracy. The commercial that they rip on President Trump about was written by myself and Stephen Miller—Stephen Miller is Jewish. There weren't any code words in that. It was off of Hillary Clinton's speech.

And this is the thing: the acid that's dropped on Trump every day about this, to try to *delegitimize* him as a president? He has not been delegitimized; he has not. This is the "nullification project," David, that started from the moment he won. The establishment rejected him, they considered him a clown, they considered *us* clowns—an island of misfit toys that ran this campaign and at least reached out to working people and said, "Yes, your concerns are our concerns." That's why we won Michigan; that's why we won Wisconsin; that's why we won Ohio. It wasn't Trump who used Barack Obama to go to places like Iowa, where he had won in landslides before, or Ohio, or these other districts; that was Hillary Clinton's campaign.

I understand how he's triggered people. That's why we may lose the house. The Left, the Time's Up movement, the resistance, and the Tom Steyer movement—I disagree with their ideology but I admire their grit and determination because they understand something that David and the Republican establishment do not get: that Donald Trump is a *transformative* president and a *historic* figure. He is going to be in your lives ten, twenty, and thirty years from now—that's a Kafkaesque novel, isn't it? It is. And it's just not about the judges and the 140 federal judges in appellate court that are going to go to two hundred, that are all going to be Federalist Society, and textualists, and originalists, and deconstruct the administrative state. It's what he's doing from a legislative point of view. Why do you think the Left has been out there like the Tea Party? Why do you think they've been out there since April and May, doing the hard work of politics, knocking on doors? You know why? They know they have to stop Trump on Tuesday or he's going to get further into their lives. They understand he's transformative; they understand he's a historical president. And it's just going to keep on.

RUDYARD GRIFFITHS: Okay, closing statements. We're going to put five minutes on the clock for you, David. And then Stephen, as per custom, you get the last word.

DAVID FRUM: I appreciate my promotion to the Republican establishment. Maybe that will help me get a reservation at the Trump Hotel where the lobbyists and the members of Congress gather to eat overpriced steaks and put money directly into the president's pocket. That seems to me pretty much where the Republican establishment is today.

If Donald Trump and the Republicans lose on Tuesday, and if they lose badly, it's not going to be because of "the Left," whatever that means. It's not going to be because of the fifty Antifa black-mask guys who roam around the United States breaking windows and committing mayhem, most of whom are probably paid police informers.

Donald Trump is going to lose because a lot of people who voted Republican in every election since 1984 — especially women — are going to say, "Enough. This is not me; this is not America."

And across Europe, one of the things that needs to be borne in mind through all of these so-called populist parties is that none of them are quite ever able to get an actual majority of the vote. They get stuck at about one-third. And the secret of their power is not democracy — not to win elections — but to manipulate the political process, to manipulate the media process, to break institutions, to take over courts, to corrupt media in order to exert power in anti-democratic ways. And that is indeed what Donald Trump has been doing in the United States: slowly corroding institutions. He is not a popular figure; populism is not popular. Populism is the art of subdividing the country and excluding much of the nation from the rest of the nation in order to justify the authority of some.

We are here tonight to talk about where the future is going, and I am going to ask you for an act of faith. I want to ask you not just to wear these poppies but to really think about what they mean, the sacrifice that earned them. We wear these to remember people who shouldered arms at a time when things seemed a lot more hopeless than they do now, a lot more frightening than they do now. In 1939, things seemed worse, and the people we were up against seemed more dangerous. And the forces of good seemed more divided — but they prevailed, and so will we. Liberal democracy is stronger than it looks because human kindness and decency are stronger than they look. The cruel always think the kind are weak. But they're going to discover that loyalty and patriotism are tremendous resources — and they are going to begin to be felt more and more.

It's been five years of a losing hand for those who believe in the things that I do, and that I hope many of you do. Whatever our party identification — whatever you call yourself — if you believe in free trade, if you believe in a free society, if you believe in an executive that's accountable to the legislature, if you believe in honest government, if you believe that the head of government shouldn't steal and do business on the side, and shouldn't be beholden to Vladimir Putin; if you believe those things, it's been five tough years. But at another dark moment, another great American president, Franklin D. Roosevelt, said, "History has recorded who fired the first shot, but in the end, all that will matter is who fires the last shot."

The future belongs to the people who cherish the future, not to the people who are despoiling it, not to the people who are indifferent, not to the people who are out for advantage, not to the people who know what they are against and can only tell you how to wreck — but to the people who actually have answers to the challenges that we as democratic societies face: the challenge of dealing with concentrated wealth, the challenge of making sure that economies grow faster, environmental challenges, the challenges of effectively and fairly governing a multi-ethnic society, the challenges of building ways that men and women can live together on terms of respect and equality. Those challenges — the people who have answers to them — the answers will always beat the non-answers. Something positive will always beat something dark. That is something, anyway, that I believe, and that I ask you to believe.

I think we are going to see, when all of this is done, that the people who have done the right thing will be able to look back on their records with pride, and the people who have done the wrong thing will not; and that the answers tonight on the other side of this aisle are heading to something that George W. Bush — for whom I worked — so memorably called "history's unmarked grave of discarded lies."

I ask you to vote *against* the resolution, but above all, *for* your faith in yourselves, in what you have built, in a better world, in a world based on mutual respect and not on the domination of some by others.

STEPHEN BANNON: That was very good, David, and irrelevant.

President Trump identified himself as a nationalist the other day, and the media went into a complete meltdown. Judge President Trump and this populist movement — and the populist movement worldwide — by their actions. Hold them accountable. We're not perfect; people are trying to figure this out as they go. But I will tell you one thing: this is about the little guy versus the elites. The little guy identifies with that, whether it's in Hungary, whether it's in Italy, whether it's in Brazil, whether it's in the United States of America. The future obviously belongs to populism. It's only going to be defined by asking if it's left-wing populism or conservative and right-wing populism; if it's about deconstructing the administrative state and opening up the power of capitalism, or about more state intervention in your entire life? *That is going to be the future.*

The battle going forward in the United States is against the Bernie Sanderses and the Cory Bookers and the Elizabeth Warrens, and that aspect of the Democratic Party that grows in strength every day — the resistance. That's the reality; the rest of it is just happy talk.

Look beyond the smears, the signal and the noise. Look at the signal, look at the actions, look at how they are bringing people in. Look at how this populist movement will reach out and take the economic nationalists and the Bernie Sanders movement. Look at how we will accommodate and bring in a third of the African-American vote in our country — something the Republican Party for decades talked about and never did. Look at it right now: I think it's 40 percent — the poll today — 40 percent of Hispanics agree with what President Trump is doing on the border, because they understand they bear the burden of the solutions of that.

I'm not saying President Trump is perfect; he wouldn't say he's perfect. He's a very imperfect instrument. He might not say he's an "imperfect instrument..."

I can understand David's frustration. I can understand the *angst,* from one of our senior public intellectuals and a leader in the Bush administration — the traditional Republican Party. Look at the fourteen people who ran against President Trump in 2016. They were the flower of a generation of donor money, of the heritage of the American Enterprise Institute, of the Cato Institute, of Paul Singer, of the Kochs — of all of it — and look at the quality of the people: Jeb Bush and Marco Rubio, Governor Christie, Ted Cruz, Rand Paul — every vertical had its best person.

It was the strongest field in the history of the Republican Party, and Donald Trump cut through that like a scythe through grass. Why? Because he talked about trade. He talked about this radical idea of free trade — particularly when you're going against a totalitarian mercantilist society like China. He talked about the deindustrialization of our country; he talked about where people's lives are; he talked about what mattered. That's why he won. That's why he won the Republican primary, and that's why he beat Hillary Clinton. Our whole thing was to compare and contrast. You, Trump, are the tribune of the people, and she is the guardian of a corrupt and incompetent elite — a permanent political class.

This is the future. And I realize David tried to demonize this — it's not racist, it's not nativist, it's not xenophobic. The "deplorables" are the finest people. We're in the Fourth Turning of American history. We had the Revolution, the Civil War, the Great Depression and World War II; and now, the Fourth Turning. Every eighty to one hundred years this happens, because in *Generation Zero* — the movie David was in with me — it's about how you're raised, how you raise the generation. We're in the great Fourth Turning. In the next ten, fifteen, or twenty years, the Unites States is either going to be the country we were bequeathed, or it's going to be something totally different. And the backbone of our country—we're not an idea; America's not an idea. It's a nation. We have the greatest land, the greatest resources; we have a divinely inspired constitution and Declaration of Independence. But that's not our strength. Our strength is the "deplorables," just like in Canada; it's the little guy. It's upon their shoulders that everything rests. And they're the backbone of the populist movement. They're not racist, they're not nativists, and they're not xenophobes. They're citizens of the greatest country in mankind's history, and *they*—not Donald Trump, not Stephen K. Bannon, not Mike Pence—*they* are going to lead us through these great turmoils to come.

Thank you very much for having us tonight.

RUDYARD GRIFFITHS: Well, ladies and gentlemen, what an absolutely superb debate. I want to start with a few thank yous. First, thank you to this audience on behalf of both of the debaters on the stage: you were engaged, you were civil—for the most part. But more importantly, I think we've done something tonight. We've shown that Toronto is capable of coming together to discuss difficult, contentious ideas in a way that informs and engages all of us, so bravo to the Munk community.

Next, I think we owe our debaters a big thank you. Let's hear it. That was superb, guys. Opinions may or may not have been changed, but both of you talked across the moral and intellectual and ideological divides in our society. And that's something that just does not happen enough, and it's a credit to this series that we were able to facilitate that tonight. So thank you, both of you.

Two final thank yous: because this was a challenging debate for everybody, there are two organizations I want to single out. First, the Roy Thomson Hall Corporation. This was not easy for this organization to pull off: they gave us this hall, they stood up for free speech, they made this debate happen! Bravo!

And finally, it goes without saying that, unfortunately, there was a demonstration tonight. I understand possibly even one police officer was injured. So I think on behalf of all of us, we just thank the Toronto Police Service for everything they've done this evening.

We are now going to vote on this resolution for a second time, and figure out how opinion has changed in this room as a result of the last hour and forty minutes of captivating debate. I'm going to open the question now, and we're going to allow you to use your clickers again. We're going to do the same thing we did last time: so, if you're in favour of the motion, "Be it resolved: the future of Western politics is populist not liberal," press *A* or the number one. If you're opposed to the motion, press *B* or the number two.

While those votes are tabulating, let's remind ourselves of where opinion in this hall started at the beginning of tonight's debate. If we can get those numbers up on the screen: 28 percent in favour of the motion, 72 percent opposed. And then we had a fairly large group of you in this hall—57 percent—that said you could change your mind.

Let's close the second vote on the resolution now. We are going to give it a few minutes to tabulate, and then we're going to find out a really important live vote at this moment: How has opinion shifted in this hall?

Summary: The pre-debate vote was 28 percent in favour of the resolution, 72 percent against. The final vote showed 28 percent in favour of the motion and 72 percent against. Given that opinion in the hall was not swayed, the debate is a draw.

Post-Debate Interviews with Moderator
Rudyard Griffiths

STEPHEN K. BANNON AND DAVID FRUM IN CONVERSATION WITH RUDYARD GRIFFITHS

RUDYARD GRIFFITHS: Steve and David, that was a terrific debate. This was an important issue, and you guys really engaged with it. On behalf of the Aurea Foundation and the Munk family, thank you for doing this.

Let's talk about a few things briefly. First of all, I like asking this question — to you first, David, and then I'll ask it to Stephen: Which of your opponent's arguments did you find the most convincing? Was there anything that Stephen said that made you think, "Hey, wow, that's a point worth registering"?

DAVID FRUM: The strongest point, and the one that is powerful to make, is the one about what people have been through over the past ten years — the pain of the financial crisis and what happened afterwards. That's really true, and that's why established institutions have taken such a beating; and, of course, the continuation of the wars in Iraq and Afghanistan. I think that really plays a big part in what's going on in the United States. And in Europe you could mention the euro crisis and the migrant crisis. Those are the powerful things that have provided the basis for this new kind of politics.

RUDYARD GRIFFITHS: Same question to you, Stephen. Which of David's arguments in this debate made you say, "Hey, that's a point worth registering; I appreciate that analysis"?

STEPHEN BANNON: Well, I actually agree with most of what he said — we have to think these things through and we have to vote. One of the reasons I came here tonight was not just to engage in the debate with the good people of Toronto. In the populist movement, if we don't convert people of David Frum's stature, as a public intellectual, we're not going to have a movement; it will peter out like he said — it burns hot and then it dies. My whole point to Republicans and particularly senior thinkers like David Frum is that, "Hey, this is an aborning movement; we need thinkers in it." I know David talked about the dark side of it, but it doesn't have to be like that. The anger that's there — the natural populist anger — can be channelled in a very *positive* direction to change the country. I thought the most impressive thing was that David is such an incredible debater.

RUDYARD GRIFFITHS: He is. Well, guys, I think we've all earned a drink. Do you agree?

DAVID FRUM: Yes.

RUDYARD GRIFFITHS: Okay, let's do it. Thanks again for a terrific debate. Thanks for coming to Toronto, Steve, David. This was a long time in the making.

STEPHEN BANNON: Thanks for having me.

DAVID FRUM: Thank you.

ACKNOWLEDGEMENTS

The Munk Debates are the product of the public-spiritedness of a remarkable group of civic-minded organizations and individuals. First and foremost, these debates would not be possible without the vision and leadership of the Aurea Foundation. Founded in 2006 by Peter and Melanie Munk, the Aurea Foundation supports Canadian individuals and institutions involved in the study and development of public policy. The debates are the foundation's signature initiative, a model for the kind of substantive public policy conversation Canadians can foster globally. Since the creation of the debates in 2008, the foundation has underwritten the entire cost of each semi-annual event. The debates have also benefited from the input and advice of members of the board of the foundation, including Mark Cameron, Andrew Coyne, Devon Cross, Allan Gotlieb, Margaret MacMillan, Anthony Munk, Robert Prichard, and Janice Stein.

For her contribution to the preliminary edit of the book, the debate organizers would like to thank Jane McWhinney.

Since their inception, the Munk Debates have sought to take the discussions that happen at each event to national and international audiences. Here the debates have benefited immeasurably from a partnership with Canada's national newspaper, the *Globe and Mail*, and the counsel of its editor-in-chief, David Walmsley.

With the publication of this superb book, House of Anansi Press is helping the debates reach new audiences in Canada and around the world. The debates' organizers would like to thank Anansi chair Scott Griffin and president and publisher Sarah MacLachlan for their enthusiasm for this book project and insights into how to translate the spoken debate into a powerful written intellectual exchange.

ABOUT THE DEBATERS

STEPHEN K. BANNON was the chief executive officer of Donald Trump's presidential campaign and served as chief strategist and senior counsellor at the White House. He was also previously a chairman of Breitbart News and a banker at Goldman Sachs. Bannon is the founder of Citizens of the American Republic, a non-profit organization that advocates for populism and economic nationalism, and is an advisor to populist leaders in the United States and Europe.

DAVID FRUM is one of North America's leading public intellectuals, a staunch critic of modern conservatism and its co-mingling with populist politics, and a former speechwriter for the George W. Bush White House. Frum is currently a senior editor of the *Atlantic* and a frequent media commentator in Canada and the United States.

He is the author of nine books, most recently the *New York Times* bestseller *Trumpocracy: The Corruption of the American Republic.*

ABOUT THE EDITOR

RUDYARD GRIFFITHS is the chair of the Munk Debates and president of the Aurea Charitable Foundation. In 2006 he was named one of Canada's "Top 40 under 40" by the *Globe and Mail*. He is the editor of thirteen books on history, politics, and international affairs, including *Who We Are: A Citizen's Manifesto*, which was a *Globe and Mail* Best Book of 2009 and a finalist for the Shaughnessy Cohen Prize for Political Writing. He lives in Toronto with his wife and two children.

ABOUT THE MUNK DEBATES

The Munk Debates are Canada's premier public policy event. Held semi-annually, the debates provide leading thinkers with a global forum to discuss the major public policy issues facing the world and Canada. Each event takes place in Toronto in front of a live audience, and the proceedings are covered by domestic and international media. Participants in recent Munk Debates include Anne Applebaum, Louise Arbour, Robert Bell, Tony Blair, John Bolton, Ian Bremmer, Stephen F. Cohen, Daniel Cohn-Bendit, Paul Collier, Howard Dean, Alain de Botton, Hernando de Soto, Alan Dershowitz, E. J. Dionne, Maureen Dowd, Michael Eric Dyson, Gareth Evans, Nigel Farage, Mia Farrow, Niall Ferguson, William Frist, Stephen Fry, Newt Gingrich, Malcolm Gladwell, Michelle Goldberg, Jennifer Granholm, David Gratzer, Glenn Greenwald, Stephen Harper, Michael Hayden, Rick Hillier, Christopher Hitchens, Richard Holbrooke, Laura Ingraham, Josef

Joffe, Robert Kagan, Garry Kasparov, Henry Kissinger, Charles Krauthammer, Paul Krugman, Arthur B. Laffer, Lord Nigel Lawson, Stephen Lewis, David Daokui Li, Bjørn Lomborg, Lord Peter Mandelson, Elizabeth May, George Monbiot, Caitlin Moran, Dambisa Moyo, Thomas Mulcair, Vali Nasr, Alexis Ohanian, Camille Paglia, George Papandreou, Jordan Peterson, Steven Pinker, Samantha Power, Vladimir Pozner, Robert Reich, Matt Ridley, David Rosenberg, Hanna Rosin, Simon Schama, Anne-Marie Slaughter, Bret Stephens, Mark Steyn, Kimberley Strassel, Andrew Sullivan, Lawrence Summers, Justin Trudeau, Amos Yadlin, and Fareed Zakaria.

The Munk Debates are a project of the Aurea Foundation, a charitable organization established in 2006 by philanthropists Peter and Melanie Munk to promote public policy research and discussion. For more information, visit www.munkdebates.com.

ABOUT THE INTERVIEWS

Rudyard Griffiths' interviews with Stephen K. Bannon and David Frum were recorded on November 2, 2018. The Aurea Foundation is gratefully acknowledged for permission to reprint excerpts from the following:

(p. 9) "Stephen K. Bannon in Conversation," by Rudyard Griffiths. Copyright © 2018 Aurea Foundation. Transcribed by Transcript Heroes.

(p. 23) "David Frum in Conversation," by Rudyard Griffiths. Copyright © 2018 Aurea Foundation. Transcribed by Transcript Heroes.

Political Correctness
Dyson and Goldberg vs. Fry and Peterson

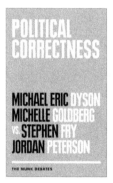

Is political correctness an enemy of free speech, open debate, and the free exchange of ideas? Or, by confronting head-on the dominant power relation-ships and social norms that exclude marginalized groups, are we creating a more equitable and just society? For some, political correctness is stifling the free and open debate that fuels our democracy. Others insist that creating public spaces and norms that give voice to previously marginalized groups broadens the scope of free speech. The drive toward inclusion over exclusion is essential to creating healthy, diverse societies in an era of rapid social change. Acclaimed journalist, professor, and ordained minister Michael Eric Dyson and *New York Times* columnist Michelle Goldberg are pitted against renowned actor and writer Stephen Fry and University of Toronto professor and author Jordan Peterson to debate the implications of political correctness and freedom of speech.

houseofanansi.com/collections/munk-debates

Is American Democracy in Crisis?
Dionne and Sullivan vs. Gingrich and Strassel

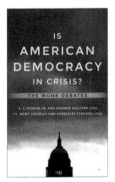

It is the public debate of the moment: Is Donald Trump precipitating a crisis of American democracy? For some the answer is an emphatic "yes." Trump's disregard for the institutions and political norms of U.S. democracy is imperilling the Republic. The sooner his presidency collapses the sooner the healing can begin and the ship of state be righted. For others Trump is not the villain in this drama. Rather, his young presidency is the conduit, not the cause, of America's deep-seated anger toward a privileged and self-dealing Washington elite. Award-winning journalist E. J. Dionne Jr. and influential author and blogger Andrew Sullivan are pitted against former Speaker of the U.S. House of Representatives Newt Gingrich and best-selling author and editor Kimberley Strassel to debate the current crisis of American democracy.

"Our country is now as close to crossing the line from democracy to autocracy as it has been in our lifetimes." — E. J. Dionne Jr.

Is This the End of the Liberal International Order?
Niall Ferguson vs. Fareed Zakaria

Since the end of World War II, global affairs have been shaped by the increasing free movement of people and goods, international rules setting, and a broad appreciation of the mutual benefits of a more interdependent world. Together these factors defined the liberal international order and sustained an era of rising global prosperity and declining international conflict. But now, for the first time in a generation, the pillars of liberal internationalism are being shaken to their core by the reassertion of national borders, national interests, and nationalist politics across the globe. Can liberal internationalism survive these challenges and remain the defining rules-based system of the future? Or are we witnessing the beginning of the end of the liberal international order?

"We can no longer confidently talk about a liberal international order. It's become disorder in the sense that democracy has been disrupted."—Niall Ferguson

The Global Refugee Crisis: How Should We Respond?
Arbour and Schama vs. Farage and Steyn

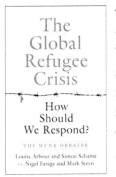

The world is facing the worst humanitarian crisis since the Second World War. Over 300,000 are dead in Syria, and one and a half million are either injured or disabled. Four and a half million people are trying to flee the country. And Syria is just one of a growing number of failed or failing states in the Middle East and North Africa. How should developed nations respond to human suffering on this mass scale? Do the prosperous societies of the West, including Canada and the United States, have a moral imperative to assist as many refugees as they reasonably and responsibly can? Or is this a time for vigilance and restraint in the face of a wave of mass migration that risks upending the tolerance and openness of the West?

"There's nothing to be ashamed of about having an emotional response to the suffering of four million Syrian refugees."
— Simon Schama

Do Humankind's Best Days Lie Ahead?
Pinker and Ridley vs. de Botton and Gladwell

From the Enlightenment onwards, the West has had an enduring belief that through the evolution of institutions, innovations, and ideas, the human condition is improving. But is this the case? Pioneering cognitive scientist Steven Pinker and influential author Matt Ridley take on noted philosopher Alain de Botton and bestselling author Malcolm Gladwell to debate whether humankind's best days lie ahead.

"It's just a brute fact that we don't throw virgins into volcanoes any more. We don't execute people for shoplifting a cabbage. And we used to."—Steven Pinker

READ MORE FROM THE MUNK DEBATES—
CANADA'S PREMIER DEBATE SERIES

Should the West Engage Putin's Russia?
Cohen and Pozner vs. Applebaum and Kasparov

How should the West deal with
Vladimir Putin? Acclaimed academic
Stephen F. Cohen and veteran journalist and bestselling author Vladimir
Pozner square off against internationally renowned expert on Russian
history Anne Applebaum and Russian-
born political dissident Garry Kasparov
to debate the future of the West's relationship with Russia.

*"A dictator grows into a monster when he is not confronted at
an early stage…And unlike Adolf Hitler, Vladimir Putin has
nuclear weapons."*—Garry Kasparov

houseofanansi.com/collections/munk-debates

*Has Obama Made the World a
More Dangerous Place?*
Kagan and Stephens vs. Zakaria and Slaughter

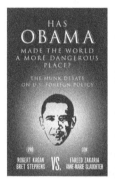

From Ukraine to the Middle East to
China, the United States is redefining
its role in international affairs. Famed
historian and foreign policy commentator Robert Kagan and Pulitzer Prize–
winning journalist Bret Stephens take
on CNN's Fareed Zakaria and noted academic and political commentator Anne-
Marie Slaughter to debate the foreign
policy legacy of President Obama.

*"Superpowers don't get to retire . . . In the international sphere,
Americans have had to act as judge, jury, police, and, in the case
of military action, executioner."*—Robert Kagan

Does State Spying Make Us Safer?
Hayden and Dershowitz vs. Greenwald and Ohanian

In a risk-filled world, democracies are increasingly turning to large-scale state surveillance, at home and abroad, to fight complex and unconventional threats. Former head of the CIA and NSA Michael Hayden and civil liberties lawyer Alan Dershowitz square off against journalist Glenn Greenwald and reddit co-founder Alexis Ohanian to debate if the government should be able to monitor our activities in order to keep us safe.

"Surveillance equals power. The more you know about someone, the more you can control and manipulate them in all sorts of ways."—Glenn Greenwald

Are Men Obsolete?
Rosin and Dowd vs. Moran and Paglia

For the first time in history, will it be better to be a woman than a man in the upcoming century? Renowned author and editor Hanna Rosin and Pulitzer Prize–winning columnist Maureen Dowd challenge *New York Times*–best-selling author Caitlin Moran and trail-blazing social critic Camille Paglia to debate the relative decline of the power and status of men in the workplace, the family, and society at large.

"Feminism was always wrong to pretend women could 'have it all.' It is not male society but Mother Nature who lays the heaviest burden on women."—Camille Paglia

Should We Tax the Rich More?
Krugman and Papandreou vs. Gingrich and Laffer

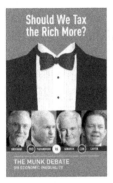

Is imposing higher taxes on the wealthy the best way for countries to reinvest in their social safety nets, education, and infrastructure while protecting the middle class? Or does raising taxes on society's wealth creators lead to capital flight, falling government revenues, and less money for the poor? Nobel Prize–winning economist Paul Krugman and former prime minister of Greece George Papandreou square off against former speaker of the U.S. House of Representatives Newt Gingrich and famed economist Arthur Laffer to debate this key issue.

"The effort to finance Big Government through higher taxes is a direct assault on civil society."—Newt Gingrich

*Can the World Tolerate an Iran
with Nuclear Weapons?*
Krauthammer and Yadlin vs. Zakaria and Nasr

Is the case for a pre-emptive strike on Iran ironclad? Or can a nuclear Iran be a stabilizing force in the Middle East? Former Israel Defense Forces head of military intelligence Amos Yadlin, Pulitzer Prize–winning political commentator Charles Krauthammer, CNN host Fareed Zakaria, and Iranian-born academic Vali Nasr debate the consequences of a nuclear-armed Iran.

"Deterring Iran is fundamentally different from deterring the Soviet Union. You could rely on the latter but not the former."
—Charles Krauthammer

North America's Lost Decade?
Krugman and Rosenberg vs. Summers and Bremmer

The future of the North American economy is more uncertain than ever. In this edition of the Munk Debates, Nobel Prize–winning economist Paul Krugman and chief economist and strategist at Gluskin Sheff + Associates David Rosenberg square off against former U.S. treasury secretary Lawrence Summers and bestselling author Ian Bremmer to tackle the resolution, "Be it resolved: North America faces a Japan-style era of high unemployment and slow growth."

"It's now impossible to deny the obvious, which is that we are not now, and have never been, on the road to recovery." — Paul Krugman

Hitchens vs. Blair
Christopher Hitchens vs. Tony Blair

Intellectual juggernaut and staunch atheist Christopher Hitchens goes head-to-head with former British prime minister Tony Blair, one of the Western world's most openly devout political leaders, on the age-old question: Is religion a force for good in the world? Few world leaders have had a greater hand in shaping current events than Blair; few writers have been more outspoken and polarizing than Hitchens.

Sharp, provocative, and thoroughly engrossing, *Hitchens vs. Blair* is a rigorous and electrifying intellectual sparring match on the contentious questions that continue to dog the topic of religion in our globalized world.

"If religious instruction were not allowed until the child had attained the age of reason, we would be living in a very different world."—Christopher Hitchens

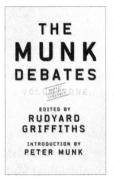